Flash Reckless

selected poems

Natasha Carthew

Published in 2002 by Onlywomen Press Limited, London, UK.

With financial support from London Arts ⠿ LONDON ARTS

ISBN 0-906500-70-2

British Library/Cataloguing-in-Publication Data.
A Catalogue record for this book is available from the British Library.

Copyright © Natasha Carthew, 2002

Typeset by Chris Fayers, Cardigan, Wales.
Printed and bound in Great Britain by JR Digital Print Services, Ltd.

For Evelyn with love.

Standing Stone, The Community of Poets Press, Canterbury, UK, 1999

Orchard Theatre Young Writers' Award – 1989
Margo Jane Memorial Poetry Prize (commendation) 1994
South West Arts Kicking Off Fund award – 2000

Royal Court Young Playwrights – Short-list – 1991
Barbican Theatre performance Ms Carthew's plays: *Amen* – 1991,
So Be It – 1992

Previous publication in:
The Rialto, Bad Poetry Quarterly, The Black Rose, Casablanca,
The Cornish Banner, Fire, Granite, Inhibition, Krax, Never Bury Poetry,
The New Writer, Otter, Pulsar, Poetry Nottingham, Speakout,
Staple (new writing), Tandem

Thanks are due to South West Arts for funding production of @16
as a booklet in 2001

Acknowledgements

Acknowledgements are due to the editors of the following publications in which some of these poems first appeared:

A4 Anonymous, Bad Poetry Quarterly, The Black Rose, Casablanca, Community of Poets Quarterly, Cornish Arts Magazine, The Cornish Banner, The Cornish Guardian, Cornwall Today, Cornish World Magazine, Fire, First Time, Granite, Inhibition, Inside Cornwall Magazine, Krax, Never Bury Poetry, The New Writer, Otter, Pulsar, Poetry Nottingham, Raindog, The Rialto, Speakout, Staple (new writing), The Sunday Independent, Tandem, The Western Morning News.

Thanks are due to BBC Radio Cornwall in which some of these poems were Broadcast.

Thanks are also due to: South West Arts for financial assistance in 2000; the Writing and Publishing consultant, Michael Williams, for his continued support over the years; and above all my Mother for teaching me that poetry exists in all things.

Contents

STORM

Storm in the air
shafts of moving sunlight
flash reckless
splash sporadic rain
into fields of too long dry
too long and heat tampered
burnt sod the colour of blind
haze is nearing
circles distant hills like prey
monuments like redundant sticks
glue themselves to a hopeful heaven
too late
the state of hell
is breathing heavy in a plastic fruit bag
filled with flies
heavy
bumbling
tired
sun is isn't
rain is sweating in a cheap crap 'pac a mac'
horizon cracks
splinters in ways and sudden glory
the dark
the wagging tree
sheets pulled to chins
sleep
cool as stars
storm is dead.

@16

At sixteen
I will act out
put down a story
glory journey
that will never seem to end
days will be hot to a burn
classrooms stenched
and hormones drenched in lust
for love
and a girlfriend
who is a friend
and a girl's kiss.

At sixteen
you discard your tights for holes
your uniform will turn to bleached crop
your imaginary tattoos will be Biro
that will draw lines and poison blood.
Blue and Amazonian.
We like to think.

At sixteen
we will leave languages for the toilets
letting authority know that
WE DON'T CARE!
For rudiments and students
and Claude, Thierry and Jean-Pierre
we sit circled and tanned
vests and tucked in skirts
and wish away the days
to the day
when you will ring me
and I will ring her
and we will run wild around rings
around time.

At sixteen
I will fail most G.C.S.E.'s
big fucking deal
I will excel at drinking
not eating
and fighting friends for fun
I will win the 100 metre dash
sell my babysitting skills for easy cash
and cocktail the rich bitch drinks cabinet
into two litre flasks.

At sixteen
school days will become lazy days
we will sit out the time it takes
for the proverbial teenage bell to toll
and then procrastinate as where to go
I want to go where she wants to go
but not where you want to go.
where should we go?

At sixteen
I want and I know I will be famous
my guitar to strum
mindless
you in your usual doped grin
humming in the bits I've not yet taught you.

At sixteen
you will have your first ****
and your first boyfriend
he will be gay
and mad
and you will love him
and leave him.
He will be called anything
and later on
everything under the sun.

At sixteen
I will make a decision
via everyone else
I will make notes
and memo hopes
I will write a story
mostly true
about me and her and them and you
strictly at sixteen.

On the last day
when barely bothered is an understatement
we shall gang down to the park
all the girls who ever were champions of cool
with tampons tied to our hair
we shall show
shall prove the oyster world
but only to ourselves.

The last gulp of warm wine
the last drag of naughty fag
smoke without fire
we belong to the school of fat chance
gobbed up with plastic spoons
and strangers' tongues
we the last lost generation
void of explanation
and classless to a fault
no joke
we the ones told we've no hope
And we know.

On the last day
of reckoning
I reckon Mrs. Parker has two heads
four fat legs
she makes us work

but I sit immersed
in mesh and clay
pissed and closeted and gay
I tell J I love her and she laughs.

On the last bell
of the last hour
I think I stay over at yours
or you at mine
leaving hoards of girly girls to cry
at the torn 'easy access' fence
they are your friends
my hopeful lovers
and we are at loggerheads
at war with the world
the odds are against us
but we will rule
we are the champions of cool.

At sixteen
summer school will become Autumn sabbatical
exiat without the 'dull do'
you will paint art like a spastic
drastic colours into a sky of blue
and she will play piano
making me fall hopelessly for her hands
finger and form
bringing me down
down to an all time low.

At sixteen
I will go to college and leave
she will go to six form and stay
and you shall not go anywhere
and will be happy there
we will be magicians of indifference
not knowing the difference

between right and wrong
and the parallel universe
that keeps us glued between.

At sixteen
I will drink you into a coma
I will punch you drunk
dislocate your jaw
yawn
and make you cry for more.

At sixteen
we will sleep in toilets
pissy concrete made for feet will be our pillow
our bed
our sheets
you will fall asleep
and wake to arthritis
and I will wake to thunder
my head my eyes my ears
you have a way of snoring me
boring me into a cubed position
submission.

At sixteen
all will go clubbing on a bus
mini
we will have no money
but lots of cheek
cheap and cheerful
kiss kiss the sailors
and buy us a bloody drink
and my best mate
and my best mate's sister
I love her
and only get drunk just to tell her.

At sixteen
I will be repeatedly kicked
my chest will lie blue and still
the dance floor will be my exampled grave
forever more
or
I will turn to run
aching to fight
and be shown
back door
and don't come back.

At sixteen
the pub will close
at half past eleven
we will have filled our skins
and chanced out unruly sins
we will stagger
cross country
and find ourselves a house
a friend of a friend of a friend
and blast our ears with early dance
grotesque romance
and hot-knives to stave off...

At sixteen
we will wake up in strangers arms
and underwear
a boy or a girl or a friend
strange
how we will come so close
to coming
to blows over who and when and why
when we rest our hearts
in each others beds
patient
and not being able to get shagging
out of our stupid pubescent heads.

At sixteen
miraculously
she will learn to swing a car
not far
but heaven and hell
and we will back ourselves in
high and mighty
singin' American pie
to the cows and heads of corn
the car will be battered
from your Mother's tipsy spins
and she will master it
with nervousness
her fingers ticking and clicking
flicking on turns of light
about corners
and me.

At sixteen
we will split our lips
dry kisses
and broken Newquay steam
bottles cracked on shallow walls
conformity fails
so much so
we even forget bottle openers
we're Queens of the lost cause
no hopers
we will laugh the stars
into oblivion
along with the jokes
splitting coppers into kicks
little shits
at sixteen.

SATURDAY EMERGENCY

Saturday emergency.
There's emergency in a Saturday night,
the eight pint wonder snake bite wife,
the whiskey women
beer baby butch
rushing the weird,
to get pissed to not remember what gets remembered
too soon
when Monday comes,
so we get the blur and it goes too quick,
too much of an emergency,
Saturday emergency,
there's emergency in a Saturday night.

LIGHT, SUNNY ROOM

It is a light, sunny room
in the room the light is sunny.
It is a room of things and the things in the room
are bright and strong and funny.

It is a large, equal square
the largeness of the square is equal.
It is a square of books and plants and books
and the books are firsts and sequels.

It is a square
above the ground in the air
in the air it is a space above the ground.
It is a two sides open space-ship and its open sides
are open to the open sound.

It is a light, sunny room
and the women in the room are funny.
It is a space where they are equal
equal in their equalness in the room that is
bright and sunny.

UNDERCURRENT

I'll follow you down
but not that far
I'll pinch that lyric
that rose
but not that boat
keeping afloat
trailing you
to where
the caves grow ice
tight
static
my might
to follow you down
but not that far
as drowning
to watch you swim
your bastard whim
and I thrash
curdled
your permanent undercurrent
give me a wave
and I'll follow you down.

DESTINY

Minor technicalities
are falling in and out of love
with the light on
three fold
fortunes have been lost
and told
wars are fought
and never won
over and over
the brakes have gone
ninety degrees downhill
falling in and out of love
destiny
a minor technicality.

WAITING

Waiting
buzzing
the mad kitchen whirr
against a thousand clocks ticking
a banging
my heart strains to wake those who are still
asleep
it's set to explode
time
I have no time for
only waiting for the bang
my aching and the door
closing around me
your arms
love
my love
calm
flat like the tide in your eyes
aqua beauty
sea that I've seen
this half-hour
waiting
this life-time
waiting
buzzing
uncontrollably
for you.

AS THE CROW FLIES

As the crow flies
the distance
between all things
the moon
the earth
and everything between
the time it takes
carriage
with a message
to follow you around the world
I will watch the sun leave
pulling in the gap of a nine hour shift
with the light
opening doors
and spreading wings
to be with you.

Across continents of dry
look to the west
of love's prevailing wind
and wish a word or two
anything
from me to you
as the crow flies
fold the distance
from there to here
just a stone's throw
between all things.

A LITTLE EDGE OF EARTH

On a little front porch
on the corner of a little edge of earth
on the other side of over here
at the opposite end of you sit reading
I sit writing
on a little hill
at the end of some lane
you are listening
I am listening to your peaceful preoccupation with
silence
the little bird
the beating heart
the storm that may or may not
in you
the sound of your God
walking fields
closing gates
is a million miles from my preoccupation with noise
the loud clatter
the running chatter
trying to keep up with your calm
your guide
your placing hands and eyes
and occasional 'shut up'
to these demanding 'whys?'.

On a little front porch
on the corner of a little edge of your heart
not so far from wherever you are
I sit writing.

A MOUTH

A mouth
is your word
against mine
your spoken grief
is my said words
before I have chance
to wait quiet
watching your mouth
lick and grip and whisper
a word
a saying
a liking to some song
some sound of happy
a smile
your silence
a kiss
a mouth.

CLOSURE

The time it takes to change your mind
or a light bulb
I will have got over you.

The time it takes to say goodbye
I will have sighed
washed all living traces
and hung them out to dry.

The time it takes to act uncertain
I will have exchanged blinds for curtains
lip service for W.I. excursions
and notes about the house will remind me
not to remember
just shopping lists
to-do lists
and lists just to say
that I have got over you.

SUCKING MARROW

Just bone
bare brittle
sucking marrow
a little
from time to time
old blood crunching
tired word munching
to death
yellow splints into brown
where white should splash red
a little
where passion seeds
spirits core opens
bare bone
old bone dry
rotting like used lust
finger tipped dust
without the marrow
bare brittle
just bone.

SUNK AT SEA
(*For Bev*)

Sunk at sea
there is no more to this
than the essence of blue
undercover
the slow of push
little by little
the turns of strait
forever
passing something
then nothing
falling
further than the sky from the earth
the heart from the mouth
the eyes closed from the fallen sunken moon
but soon
more than this
the rising tide
the taste
the smell
the sound
of land
passing the things that need not be
out at sea
swimming.

SHOOTING FOR THE MOON

Shooting for the moon
see the sudden clouds burst
exploding wisdom
fractal
in a silver sky.

Stretching for the stars
the biggest
watch them shoot from sight
complicating wishes
in a mumbled after thought
too late.

Calling to the birds
fastest spirits of calm
hear them bid goodnight
farewell
all eyes of rush and freedom
an ultimate Kingdom
without distraction
just being
and able
shooting for the moon.

THE SOUND OF TREES

The sound of trees
pulling roots to rockets
to the sky
the only thing to hold the wind
to make of it fading
leaving
making distance
the pull of rain
from another sky
sound of fast
past to future
just here
the sound of open
stretching possibilities
the ground as protector
the sound of trees.

FATHER

You're a preacher now,
you love the attention and how,
the bible to your right hand,
and you like to bash.
Father
I believe you like to bash,
do you?

You're a red neck now,
out in the sticks,
lighting fires,
little cute ones for the kids,
big daddy likes to build big fires,
big daddy with KKK stamped to his chest.
You're a father,
father,
second time around,
playing pick up sticks out in the yard,
waiting until dusk,
I bet you like to bash,
playing bashing sticks with me,
it could be me.

Father.

You're a preacher now,
so saintly,
on the wagon,
off the drugs,
preacher preaching preacherly,
tell them your daughter's a dyke
daddy
tell them you're my father,
preacher,
you're my father.

OUT

When I like out
the rains come
a big purple cloud as my hat
a river of grey for my shoes.

When I go out
the sun stays shade
and fades
the fields marsh me
march me to the nearest swinging tree
help me.

When I come out
the moon will hold my face
smiling
taken in view
of all the names and all the taunts
won't haunt me
when I like out
I will go out
I will shout
to the lilac rain running
to the yokels pointing
I am out.

SUMMER OF NO RETURN

This is the summer of no return,
these are the long languid days that melt
and open like streams to the sea.
Here is the clock that ticks over but is not noticed,
the warm thunder nights that spit occasional rain
but then again,
this is the summer that toasts us without threat,
these last days of innocence versus some pending pain.

These are the fruits and foods that mother cooks,
the table spread into the garden and out onto the lawn,
this is the cider allowed to drink in public at last.
Here are the friends that stole boats, made fires and
                                        camped out
'till dark with us,
here the heart shaped stone that someone gave to
                                        someone else,
and here the tree that broke most legs,
knife carved names scratched up to it's belly
and here the old rope swing,
swinging but ready for fall.

Here is the path up into the cliffs,
the bare foot slip and cut
initiating our small minds, ways and tricks,
here the trees arch and dot shade into night
whispering as the day melts,
this is the last day of summer,
this is the summer of no return.

CORN BELT

Will I wear it or walk it?
Think about it or do it?
Shave my head with dread
or brush it long for peace sake
keep sake in a bag
shorn
or pinned up to remind others
of my unhappy childhood
sillyhood
such a pretty girl
but never happy or good
I wear my Cornish name
my badge
my gun in my rural neighbourhood
where I scare and am sometimes scared
to tell all
feel and felt
sky blue
sea yellow
corn belt.

BATH WITH CANDLES

There was a riding,
horseback through the water and down amongst the fog,
the turns were strait,
across the hills and down past the well,
the wooded brook and dark, dense forest,
and the mountains that grew from nowhere
then shortened in an instance,
sailing the rider hopefully to the openings,
the suns.
In each fade of darkness she took to being home,
where the orange cracked and stripped it's warmth
from bow to stern.
The pleasure was just bearable there,
there where she'd spoil up her boat and take to landing,
the yellowed grass and silver rivers,
amongst the heat and two way traffic
there was a riding,
horseback through the water,
to the openings,
the suns,
where she found home.

KNOWING WITHOUT DOING

There is nothing to write about but to write about the
                                                    weather
the cold blasts of rain across the plains of hot heather
the sun in it's smiling and the bare noses burning
and the little ants
the bloody ants that keep on biting.

There is nothing to think about
but to think about the thinking
the should we's and shan't we's and the little bits of
doing without knowing and knowing without doing.
She cooks
I write and think about how she wants me to cook.

There is nothing to say but to say what you want
I want
I don't want and you certainly don't want.
I say the grass is green but on closer inspection
we know the dogs have been
and I just say what I say just to say it.

There is nothing to write
but to write what I would write
if I could be bothered to write.
And then the sun's down
and she's chopped the mushrooms
and I stop writing what I think and start
doing without knowing and knowing without doing.

PLANT

Deadly poisonous
this plant looks like love
smells like hardship
tastes like death
this sweet tastes like bitter
without the froth
this head
dangling flower thorn red
waves happy hello's
sorrow goodbyes
sending wreaths like vultures to grave's end
round the bend and back again
this plant sups loony juice
fermented rain and slush from casual seas
deadly poisonous
planting love but looks deceive.

PEARL

Beached
submerged
a stone's throw
from what I know
the coming of a shape
getting closer
closing
within reach.
Smooth to my touch
like skin bumping skin
a shape that goes around
tapers
a touch echoing smoothness
inside
a pearl
precious hiding place
a cupped cave
wet and warm.

Watching
a flash of rainbow in my hand
past glories reflected
of other nights and other's stories
kissing memories into my skin
placing the sandy grains of time
between us
ocean bound
leaving me with the taste of salt on my hand.

DEEP DARK DOWN

I left my identity down by the sea
lost my mind
my muted words
all sculptured love I left on land
my horizontal scope
a rising tide.

I left my suitcase high up on the rocks
years of hard co-ordination
a scatter of therapy
colouring every mood to find me
hand-me-downs that shackled being free.

I left my caring across the white-washed village
the towering cliffs that urged me to fall
friends and foe and everyone pushing
each with my eyes my hair my frown
an ocean of cousins.

I left down by the sea
neatly sat my shoes
and thrashed to a swim
floated everything
into the deep dark
I left my identity.

WHITE SUMMER

Nothing inspires.
Damp bleached grass
crippled rose-petals drooling
the steaming city spitting sweat
the rains came, wept and went.

Nothing transpires.
Just a smeared white sun
daisies pop soggy flip-flop heads
and what stretches through thirst then dies
growing, drying dead.

Nothing fires.
Passion yawns achingly
birds lie on backs and gurgle routinely
a phone rings and rings still
the sun comes, burns and wrecks.

DIM CITY

Dim city
churning
chugging noise
into fumes
into smoke
turning warmth into suffocation
sunshine into Hiroshima clouds.

Grey palette
hinting yellow and brown
grim and shitty
then darkness
sooty
and only one two stars
but not in the sky.

Bursting blunder
pelting tastes
solid dusty drops
flops
a sloppy intake
shallow half-breath
churning guts
chugging hic-ups
down like underground
buried in dim city.

FIERCE

Fierce
is the wild man
in my feminine sheep's clothing
fierce
is the brave-heart
hard unhurt
fierce
is the cutting out of tongue
through hunger
fierce is the jolt of shock
that puts fight above fear
fierce is the stronger
wild stranger
captain of a blood bath mutiny
suicidal beauty
fierce is the winning
brimming with passion
psychologically damaged
but will manage
can't see the wood for the trees
in here
fierce.

EXECUTION

I don't believe in public execution
exhibition
two genital balloons
and a slim volume of verse
it's perverse
to be microphoned
and microscoped
into hope for a two pound fifty sale
holds nothing but pointlessness
and word betrayal
I don't believe
another art
rips out the heart
in quite the same way
but the silly poet
and the silly poem
self-righteous or nervous
in a silly sickly sweet sauce
plants a cherry on the head of words
that have lived and lasted
on the page for a lifetime
not days
is what I believe
is something more than personal
execution
is not a cold public hall
but a corner of some moment
of some day
of some time
that takes the heart in two hands
and with a whisper
mouths the words of
mother
daughter
lover

and laughs
and holds
and cries.

WORK IS

Work is
the stiff scratching of spine
tense and brittle to a break
the open heart
surgery
hardened to a hurt
letting closeness in
and then pushed around
grounded into chores of disillusion.

Work is
soft lifeless muscles
walking the same corridor
past the same grey suit
lifeless bag
in foot after obedient foot
carrying vaguely
but not to any particular goal.

Work is
my face is lifeless
drawn on tracing paper
charcoaled and rubbed to a blur
unnoticed
smiling at strangers
just to make them feel good
my hollow eyes
my hollow cheeks
my hollow life.

Work is
what is left of time
and money
'end of the month' hurry
to buy things we no longer need

careless greed
grabbing at leisure implements
the implementation of having
but never having the time for doing.

Work is
bringing me to my knees
an all time ever so low
hold
two skinny arms wrapped
to keep body in place
when all around is starting to fold.

INTRODUCING . . .

Pub culture
slow as a stick
the glimmer of cracked ashtrays
the shine to a burn of wood
glistening to a dirty gleam
through
windows fagged with country smog
shit and silage and sewage splashed
trucks hauling and howling for easy cash
in hand
and fast
pub vultures
girls with rubbed, stitched and pierced bellies
getting the wash in whilst avoiding pay
all light and weary and wearing
eyes bossed and smiling
flashing
dead
pub monsters
drunks drunk and crawling
calling to barmaid babs
titty tycoon
slabs for flab
please please
as honest as a cheat
gets paid next week
and the next week
rain has changed to steam of hot
stools are pulled to closed doors
plastic chairs to road edge
only a little too adventurous
and far from the bar
pub culture
sit on my lap and I'll dance you a song

look no hands
give us a light and I'll steal it
up to the moorland
gypsy camp where no one treads
but fears
in this year
reminiscing on last year
planning to go sober
next year
happy new year
pub culture
sing a ring a silly song
Scottish shite or such
so much fuss for little more than a hangover
empty pockets
empty soul
fighting young until liver failure
then dead or old
too lethargic to care or moan
to friends
enemies
social standing higher or lower
and further
deeper
conversations that echo
and beg the stupid question 'Why are we here?'
pub culture
be my buddy if I be yours
old fucked bastard
cry on my shoulder
and it is too late
and you are a waster
living the Vida lost hoper
come on
in
live the life of brawl and sin
the ultimate ultra fun themed hole

open for business
our legal drug hustler
ladies and gentlemen
we give you
pub culture.

THE DRUG AND AIDS GENERATION

We're the drug and AIDS generation,
no pearly whites slashing like in the seventies,
silky flares and disco stomps.
Didn't they have it all?
And they say we've got it easy.

Mass crowds on a Saturday night,
everything starts with an E
apparently.
Drugs just 'cause
'cause we can,
we can.

Heavenly haven toilets,
a quick shag up against the bloody tiles,
slipping on the floor,
piss wet through.
We're the aniseed ball and tizer generation,
we were,
the flavoured lip gloss and wash-in wash-out.
Now the sherbet's just for snorting,
if you can afford it.

The don't pretend sixties extension,
no more the rose-coloured glasses,
everything's very clear,
clear and present,
like at school in registration,
who's missing?
Then it was called bunking,
now it's called death.
We're the drug and AIDS generation,
knowone's pretending.

SITTING

Sitting
not giving in to motion
photo in hand
of you sitting
not giving in to motion.
Your face
one beautiful dimension
times three
each shadow
each fade of light
I see you sitting
against this roomed backdrop
wombed as you know it so well.
You're laughing
and I laughed framing your smile
in a tilt
your head crowned with a pointed hat.
You told me to hide it
burn it
toss it like caution to the wind
but I have it here
giving in to my emotion
it lies in my hand
sitting.

ROUTE

Walk with me
whilst I walk with you
these stumbling times
talk to me
trees and wind and rain
all mumbling lines
your face your voice your mind in my mind.

Sit by me
and I'll sit silent by you
this wintry day
circle me with hush
brush my cheek with soft and salty
all whispered love
chewing any news to touch me.
Be near me
and I'll be near to you
with coming years
know me
and I know you will
all given fears to winter
paths and routes and crossroads
walk with me.

STANDING STONE

Standing stone,
this me that leans hard
but sits as soft as moss,
I alone that hates but loves just as much,
towering to all but then pebble small,
this me who crumbles to dust in any kind of fall,
here the hardship,
cold lipped and bold,
I alone standing stone.

FUNERAL

A length of lane I have not yet walked
the depth of sea I'll glance at
my whole life coasted to a ball.
The relatively known face that I will echo
the wide eyes and choking smile
all the while
steps that step no beat
and hands that clutch unlucky charms
of not much
a gift from love to life
from old to young way back when.

A stretch of wood I did not build
a scratch of words rubbed out
unsaid
these fields
these hills
all trees that ache with age
leaning towards your final page
character finds setting but falls to the plot
this land
this earth
runs a length of lane I have not yet walked.

BROWN TREE, GREEN GRASS

Because the world thinks I'm wierd
because the carpet was swept
under feet fast
because all I was left with
brown tree, green grass
because the earth
did not stand still
for me
did not move
with me
because the world shouts me odd
for the passion to be bothered
to be moved by silly slugs sucking salt from my toe
because lovers do not
understand love as I know
given like plague in a wrapper
fatal
addictive
can be so easily taken away
because simple life is all
being being endlessly being
because I understand
all there is
beautiful and worthy of hurt
is brown tree, green grass.

WALKING MAPS

Walking maps.
Plain blue rivers catch
imaginations
scaled exaggerations
but then cuts creases like bombed out towns.

Fingering thumb taps.
String stretching inches
then frayed to the sea
empty
no miles
but five miles miling five mile squared.

Scratching printed mock-ups.
Roughly A plus B means motorway
running scared
bared of trees
and paper thin.

THE END OF THE DAY

At the end of the day
close all these doors
make the kettle hot
draw all curtains
make certain
that what is done is done
what is said is said
the sky has darkened
put all arguments
contradictions
to bed.

WILL

I should type out every single line
every word every rhyme
place heart in piles and soul in files
lettered A to Z and back
littered like useless leaves
pages upon pages of me.

I shall list first lines like lost lives
gravestones grey and spoken for
each carve an old carve and much like the last
written as if spoken but hidden under ivy
like death threats, death notes and poison pen etchings
binned and burned and all anything left unsaid.

I will write as meant to write
and the pauses in between
mouthing love in a dusty shoe-box
brimming wrinkles and attic bound
lying lonely and fading furiously
words that caused and barely stirred
tie a big pink ribbon and place a smile
and write my will with a kiss.

ISLAND

Dusting doorstep
the clean arch
butted like an island
beautiful
as the butt-ends surround
building
then the doorstep is dusted.

The clean arc
a rain washed rainbow
dragging us back
to the sea
our backs against the sea
where we belong
setting sail
me playing at the helm
you
looking stern
cleaning the arc.

Like an island
but
we grow up
around each other
expanding
new love
a life time
and several centuries finding
each other
beautiful
this island we like.

WILD WEST

Wild
the west is unforgiving
bare back
the lonely acres of high
the dust of devils
the thirst of gorse
wild
and strangely unlived in
the mile that is trekked
against backdrop of half a day
the circle of travel
unravel cold protection down to bare bone
dismount to
the heat of ancient stone
the dry and the burning
hands and brow
throw the rope
catch the sun and bring it down
the west is bushfire burning
hurting
walking wounded
running wild.

FATE

Just because
I'm arrogant now
doesn't mean
I was arrogant when
the moon was in
'open all hours'
in my sun sign
way back then
when the stars gathered
pondered on fate
and decided it was too late
to make of me anything
but an anyone
walking the lanes
in pain
just like another shadow
just because.

DEATH OF A TOURIST

Escape
to the cold crust of earth
grey blue bruise
slip
rockpool fools
elope
to the crisp crack of rock
shit
slope
shock
zero ground
down
to the cave grave
of won't be found
waiting
bait to the hook
line and blinkered
look to the camera
smile
here comes the wave.

THE RIPPED TIDE

The ripped tide
beauty gashed into so much blue
blood of glory
the clot and plot of story
uncertainty
not true.

The river rides
a thousand hiding places
memories
faces
hands cupped and drunk
splashed and washed
dirty clean
gleam of trance
the sun rising
moving horizon
throwing colour into trees of branch
breaking
early into afternoon
blue to green
cut into memory like so much wedding cloth
the soft and curl
barnacle laced
small world
steps washed without trace.

The ripped tide
open wide
say ahh
for the child who bleeds salt water
gleamed from the sea
the mermaid mother
serpent father
fish out of water daughter.

The inner river guides
gathers chaos into brooks
open book
reads like an idyllic childhood
the pleasure played
mapped out treasure and traps
the heat of sun and tight of gripped lapping laughter
blue bath slaughter
as lonely and as painful as beauty
gashed into my smile
my eyes
the ripped tide.

Onlywomen Press, Ltd.
Feminist Lesbian publishers since 1974

Website: www.onlywomenpress.com

Most UK, European, Australian and
US bookshops either carry our books in stock
or can order them for you.

Alternatively, for a free mail-order catalogue
of our poetry, fiction and non-fiction,
send your name and address to:
Onlywomen Press, Dept. FC,
40 St. Lawrence Terrace,
London W10 5ST, England.